THROUGH THE EYES OF A FLAME

Poems of Past Loves and Past Lives

CAMILA CARRILLO

Copyright © 2024 by Camila Carrillo

All rights reserved.

NO PART OF THIS BOOK MAY BE REPRODUCED IN ANY FORM OR BY ANY ELECTRONIC OR MECHANICAL MEANS, INCLUDING INFORMATION STORAGE AND RETRIEVAL SYSTEMS, WITHOUT WRITTEN PERMISSION FROM THE AUTHOR, EXCEPT IN THE CASE OF BRIEF QUOTATIONS EMBODIED IN CRITICAL ARTICLES OR REVIEWS.

Cover design and Illustration by Angela Mai

THIS BOOK IS PROTECTED BY COPYRIGHT LAWS. UNAUTHORIZED DISTRIBUTION OF THIS BOOK, IN PART OR IN WHOLE, IS STRICTLY PROHIBITED.

PREFACE

This collection emerged during moments of grief and joy, each poem serving as a stepping stone toward healing. I hope these words find those who need them, as they once found me

For all, on Earth and in the cosmic realm of creation.

REMEMBER YOU ARE LOVED:

"Sweet child lingering in the depths of darkness, with a mind so bright, radiating through every soul and every heart. Witnessing a remarkable nature in a world so cruel yet so kind.
You wonder the answers that lie beneath the surface because you know there's more than ever imagined.
Don't sit and wait for a moment, contemplating the what if's.
Life is so fragile, so precious. just a grain of sand within a billion universes in such an ordinary world."

CONTENTS

To You From Me — xiii

1. INTERTWINED — 1
   SEA — 1
   SPRING — 2
   222 — 3
   RENEWAL — 4
   REMINISCING — 5
   333 — 6
   ASHES — 7
   WAX & HONEY — 8
   REBIRTH — 9
   HERE NOW — 10
   DECEMBER — 11
   FRAGILE — 12
   ADAM AND EVE — 13
   FLIPSIDE — 14
   AUGUST — 15
   FALL — 16

2. SHEDDING — 18
   LA — 19
   EGO — 20
   APOLOGY — 21
   LIMERANCE — 22
   MAGNOLIA — 23
   HOMESICK — 24
   ALCHEMY — 24
   MELANCHOLIA — 25
   TENDER — 26
   CONONDRUM — 27
   HUMAN — 28

DOUBT	28
PRESENCE	29
FORGIVENESS	30
PARADOX	31
NIRVANA	32
GAIA	33
FIRE BIRD	34
PART 2	35
3. A CHAPTER OF HEALING	36
APPLE TREE	37
INNOCENCE	38
VESSEL	39
PART 2	40
SATURN HAS RETURNED	41
CHAOS	42
TENDER	43
HEAVIER THAN HEAVEN	44
TEATHER	45
GENESIS	46
POLARITY	47
REKINDLE	48
BROKEN	49
4. TRANSMUTATION	50
EARTH ANGEL	50
ETHER	51
LIGHT BEING	52
ESSENCE	53
INCARNATION	54
APHORDITE	55
PARIS, TEXAS	56
WINGS YOU DESIRED	57
ILLUMINATION	58
CHEMISTRY	59
TRANSUMITING	59
FRAGMENTS	60

RESURRECTION	61
EPIPHANY	62
FINALE	63
...	65
About the Author	67
Notes	69

TO YOU FROM ME

Words can often be a vulnerable experience, a verbal expression, true to some and heard by many.

These are mine. Sharing to be felt, taken in and offering a helping hand along this little journey we call life.

I
INTERTWINED

SEA

There's a warmth I feel whenever I lay eyes on you
An ocean tide deep inside the furthest layer of my heart
    you've yet set to sail

I know you want to unravel every part of my mind and
    every inch of my soul
I am terrified of the tide that's buried beneath my surface

Every time you're near me I want to let you in but the
    past resurfaces
and a light starts to dim

You've captured me with your essence
And a spark of hope
I think we're all searching for someone,
something more

CAMILA CARRILLO

SPRING

Whenever my mind lingers to the very thought of you
It takes me back to the cold rain in April and the warm
    breeze of May
A softness so still time stops and suddenly I'm there again

How do we forgive those we can't forget?
How do we heal a heart that's already been broken?

A constant reminder for a gentle soul
Searching for every answer
When the only answer is buried within her

222

"I just want to feel your warmth" he said

NOT KNOWING SHE'D BE THE GREATEST FIRE HE WOULD EVER BURN

CAMILA CARRILLO

RENEWAL

Tender warm bodies
Longing for a touch that is no longer present
In a world that once was
A dream so far away now turned to dust

Why must we yearn for ghosts of our past selves?

When we can become alive again

REMINISCING

In the depths of great silence and solitude
I longed for you ever endlessly
Time passed yet the only presence I felt was yours
Still lingering after all that was said and done
The words you spoke echoed through the distant memo-
   ries we once shared

A vision now
Only seen in my dreams where we still reside
How I wish to start over knowing what I know now

Promising to never let you slip
under the roof of my palms
And touch of my fingertips

333

To be loved is an illusion in one's own memory

Just like being felt is as real as a dream in our imagination

ASHES

*He ran his fingers through my hair on a warm
    summer day
I thought I saw his eyes they were begging me to stay
I felt so at peace, content and at home
Maybe you might've missed me*

or maybe you felt alone

*He planned his return and we made amends
Breaking me once wasn't enough for you so you had to do
    it again*

*Understanding is in my nature while kindness is my
    whole
But stepping in my fire*

Will only burn your soul

CAMILA CARRILLO

WAX & HONEY

We'll melt together
For the only thing we've ever know was each other
Recognizing our endless endeavors
The highs, the lows, the beauty and pain.
We are who we are
Two fragile beings
Lost between time & space

Never wanting you more than I do now

REBIRTH

Cocoons shedding their skin to be reborn again
I shed mine when I first met you,

A beautiful butterfly, without its wings

CAMILA CARRILLO

HERE NOW

I am a soul
Present to many and seen by few
Capturing fragments in the eyes of those who speak
And lips that quiver when spoken

DECEMBER

I saw you entangled within the ropes of my being
An eternal sunshine clouded in dark thunder and misty fog
I swore I knew you, just like you knew me
Reembarking new journeys
Separate paths in order to start again
Reminiscing
Feeling these long cold nights
Where the only warmth I needed was not found in my weighted blanket
But within the weight of your very presence

The greatest feeling of them all

CAMILA CARRILLO

FRAGILE

We come across those we hurt
In order to repair the broken fragments already inside
    of us
Projecting deep rooted insecurities, fears

Shielding ourselves from the love we receive
While accepting a momentary love we think we deserve

ADAM AND EVE

I un-tied these blue ribbons that held me so tightly
Those ribbons once made of haywire
Sharp and cold
As icy as your heart became
Before your softness slipped and withered away

I saw you underneath the apple tree
But the only Adam I pictured was you

Enticing snakes crawling from the avenues of the green valley
Enticing your ripened mind
So tender and pure

Innocence was lost
Innocence was gone

We cry to those we love
In order to love those we hate
AND STILL, WE CHOOSE PAIN
Instead of embracing the warm hollow light
In which we come upon

An energy beyond knowingness
But knowing you
Was the only light I'd ever known

CAMILA CARRILLO

FLIPSIDE

I saw you in every face I came across
A ghost within reality
A tangibility so sweet
I wanted you to see me for who I was
Not for who you wanted me to be
There were two sides to every story
But the story was mine

While you belonged to no one

AUGUST

Tender lover
Caressing my skin with the sweetest touch
Gentle eyes
I won't forget

You are a memory
Everlasting in the depths of my fragile heart
And wavering mind

While tracing my fingers through the curls of your hair
You whispered to me
"I'm glad I met you"
As the echo in my head replied

If only we could've met sooner

CAMILA CARRILLO

FALL

Old ghosts resurfacing in the shadows of my heart
And as the leaves kept falling,

So, did we

2
SHEDDING

*We are constantly shedding old skin in order to
rebirth again
transforming into butterflies gilded by its wings
soaring into new heights*

*And with every chapter,
We evolve into the light we are derived from and the
gentle darkness that awaits our bones*

LA

Encapsulated sunshine
Hidden beneath the array of your aura
Bright and gloomy
Another rainy day in LA
We live and breathe for these moments that keep us sane

But I will never be as perfect as you want me to be
There is no such thing

I am me,
And you are you
Living simultaneously
It's just us two

CAMILA CARRILLO

EGO

My kin
My heart
My kindred soul half
I searched and longed for ever endlessly

I'm scared of breaking you apart, because other parts of me have shattered long ago

APOLOGY

So this is what it's like
When asked if a stranger has ever changed your life?

How could I have known you so deeply
Yet still know nothing at all

Those sapphire eyes
They have this hold on me
Deeper than the deepest ocean
Another mystery
I can't seem to explain

But I know you can't either

CAMILA CARRILLO

LIMERANCE

I loved you
Sometimes love is never enough,

We can try holding on to what is familiar
What feels the most comfortable
The most right

But comfort turns into dependency

And my need for you was pain

MAGNOLIA

I live in this dream reality of mine
Far away from my thoughts
And close to my bed

Tonight, I give myself to you
Then tomorrow
I'm free again

CAMILA CARRILLO

HOMESICK

How could I be such a fool to think
That a heart like mine
Could ever forget a heart like yours?

ALCHEMY

I envy those around you
As they get to witness magic
In such human form

MELANCHOLIA

No time to think and no room to ponder
Rather these nights were often melancholy
This feeling bittersweet
As sweet as you once were to me

Juice dripping from the roof of my mouth
Down towards these tender lips of mine
Mangoes that are still ripe

A summer fruit
Reminiscent of winter
Maybe even spring
Only you knew that

And a part of me hopes you still do

CAMILA CARRILLO

TENDER

White lace covers my body
Sheer tights made of delicacy
Almost as delicate as I am
As delicate as I claim to be

I paint my nails crimson cherry red
And my eyes of indigo blue
Hiding away from a reality I never seemed to escape
Nor did I ever want to

Emotions that could sing
Feelings that echo through these forgotten walls
A burning rage that breaks them down

So tell me now
Who are you?
When there's no one else around?

CONONDRUM

We give
So we can receive
And still we take without giving

Life is a mystery worth living but to live is a gift on its own

CAMILA CARRILLO

HUMAN

> I find solace in knowing that a constant struggle
> Is a temporary battle
> In a mind so heavy and restless
> Waiting for a sweet lullaby
> I only remembered at the age of six
>
> Childlike innocence
> Now innocently gone
>
> How I wish to be carried away in my bed
> And for a moment have these lingering thoughts
> laid to rest

DOUBT

> Salty tears fell every night
> Forgetting who I was and who I was made to be
> Another storm
> Imperfectly perfect
> Skin and bones
> Just like your body
>
> You say we are different
> Yet we remain the same
>
> A tethered soul
> Waiting to be found in the midst of our glory

PRESENCE

Please tell me now how this chapter ends
So I can finally lay your memory to rest

Can't you see?
Death does not haunt me
Nor does it enthrall me

But a piece of you always will

CAMILA CARRILLO

FORGIVENESS

You said you loved me
When everything you've ever loved wasn't me at all

What you lived for
Was everything I could never be

I tried so hard to fill this mold and emptiness you left
     behind
Shaping myself to become someone I thought you wanted

And what you wanted was never me

PARADOX

She melts like trees in a forest fire
Trail blazing all she left behind
Everything worth caring for
A painted picture of who she used to be
A distant memory that cannot be found

How can she be so many versions of herself to so many different people?

Who is she and where did she come from?

No one will ever know
And neither will I

CAMILA CARRILLO

NIRVANA

Heaven and Earth collided when you were born
A mystical sense of self
An eternity of being for decades
Maybe even centuries ago

Who are you?
And who am I?

The universe surrounds us
We are one
As we are many
Purifying this earthly world

GAIA

Mother, I am lost by your beauty
And haunted by your past
Who dares to bring life in this darkened world?
I simply cannot bear

Your strength inspires me
It provokes me
We are two as we are one

But I am not you

                Nor will I ever be

CAMILA CARRILLO

FIRE BIRD

I want to be free
Maybe more like myself

This unholy mess of chaos
I can't seem to escape or runway from has me wrapped in
   its arms
Relying on the comfort of familiarity
As we usually do

What is my purpose? I ask
If creation is obsolete
And beauty is desire

I live for expression
I'm here for the truth
I am the muse behind your story
As you are mine
We fuel each other

When the fire burns and the ashes thicken
A phoenix rising
Here I come
I AM BORN AGAIN

PART 2

I belong to everyone
As I belong to no one

I am here
I am present
But I am there
And I'm not

Like a bird
Sailing away
You cannot tame me
You shall not free me
I am already as free as they come
So don't try and rescue me

   For I am almost extinct!

❦ 3 ❧
A CHAPTER OF HEALING

*Raw emotions are real emotions
Waiting to be released*

APPLE TREE

You gave me your seed
A ripened fruit
I never asked for
Bitterness with temptation
Pleasure
Without remorse

CAMILA CARRILLO

INNOCENCE

A mother's milk
Consumes the starving child in need of affection
A void left to be filled
Heard like mentality
Raised by wolves
He was only a sheep

Shepard please come
We are in dire need
Thirsty for flesh
Only left to breed

Clenching teeth sinks in her skin
Blood-soaked sheets

She is all he needs

When she has left
Who will he be?
A mother's child, who was once foreseen

VESSEL

My body is tense
Cold as a winter breeze
When you are near me
Shivers run through my spine
You steal my warmth
And leave me dry
Evaporated blood
Soaked in bleach

It's what you do
It's who you are

Now go on
Deplete me
Then dispose me as you do best

Another victim of your own demise
No empathy
No virtue left inside

"Leave me alone" I say,
"Leave me to die."

PART 2

An entity made of distortion
Blood milk
I'm thirsty
Sour breath decays
I steal your soul
You take my existence away
You still don't know me and you never will

Don't pretend like you do
Don't pretend that you care

Humans like us will vanish into thick smoke and thin air
Gone as the wind that carries me away

Goodbye
For I will rest another day
Goodbye
I will rest and decay

SATURN HAS RETURNED

A vessel of lies
A blind masculinity
Hiding in his own tragedy

Shame, shame
They forgave you
Shame, shame
She who raised you

A begotten son
Reproduction waste
You threw her away
Burned her down
Burned at the stake
Real love
Now turned to waste

How dare you kill her for some nickels and a dime?

Don't be a fool
Don't sell yourself cheap
Those who sin, will sin again

Karma comes and goes
Karma comes in three's
At twenty-seven
or thirty-three

CAMILA CARRILLO

CHAOS

Humans without awareness
Enforcing their beliefs

A righteous state of being
Beings with no righteousness

Fighting for morality
In an immoral world

How do we cleanse ourselves?
And how do we cleanse this life?
Please tell me now so I can sleep in hope of a restful night

TENDER

Sensitivity lingers through my body
I want to know who you are
So I can delve into the deepest parts of your mind and see
    if I'm anywhere to be found

If there's a lack of empathy
I want to know why

I want to unravel the truth that cloaks itself around you
It cloaks around me too
I still let it see light
I know there's a light somewhere

People remain hidden in order to stay in the dark
The sun is too bright for them

Warmth is all I've ever known
It's all I've ever been and everything I want to be
I don't understand and I never will

It brings me comfort in knowing I will never be like you
Even when I don't want to be me either

CAMILA CARRILLO

HEAVIER THAN HEAVEN

Something to die for
Another sacrificial debt now washed clean
A chapter unwritten
A story left undone

We laughed at the what ifs not knowing they'd soon become a what now?

A price to pay
Heavier than my soul
Heavier than yours too

TEATHER

Go on and go there
My sweetest child
You're a garden I planted
Created in my head
Rooted in my own mind
To be watered and destroyed

I'll fade away
So you can remain

This creation
So pure and holy
I was once her too

Now all that is left
Is plotting soil and a dying tree

CAMILA CARRILLO

GENESIS

Golden locks
Were Intertwined
Breed me
I shall breed again
Leave me
You can leave again

A part of me
Now half full and left to be empty
Broken limbs
Tear me to pieces
It's nothing new

My angel,
Heaven only waits for you
It rings its bells
And clears its skies
A simple hello makes another goodbye
Never far your always near

Guiding light
Please stay right here

POLARITY

Your eyes saw my beauty like I never did
They saw my body undressed
Unraveled in your sheets as I lay beside you

Hearts beating
Anxiety ran its course

You said you felt safe around me
So why couldn't I?

Now your eyes only see the pain
That I can't feel
I just see you
And all the bruises marked on my body
The many scars that won't ever heal
But I'll go on, so I can forget you
Even when I don't want too

Your memory is a reminder of my own remorse and
    there's nothing left for you to see

Nothing left inside of me

CAMILA CARRILLO

REKINDLE

*The light you saw within me has turned into a burning
   fire
Flames once bright golden red
Now into solemn shades of blue
Heavy smog and thick ashes are all that remain
And so is this tragic reminder of you*

*Warm embers
Will only burn if we let them
Still, it's never enough to fuel a flame
That has extinguished
Before it could even begin*

BROKEN

My body is a glass tempered mirror
Delicate and fractured with a tough exterior
Ready to shatter its pieces and cut you open

I'll bleed from the same blood I've traded
And for the worn-out clothes
Laid on your bedroom floor

Those faces linger
And never go away

I'll trade myself for an empty night of promises and a half
*   glass of wine you poured me*
Taking something that was never yours to begin with

Everyone wants a piece of the same cake you so selfishly
*   devoured*
Go on, take another piece
So that nothing is left of me

Please, oh please
I am only sweetness if you let me be

4
TRANSMUTATION

EARTH ANGEL

Light bearer
You transmute all my darkness
Into golden rays of colors i've never seen before
Others only dreamt of

You come into my world
And wash me clean
My sins are now forgiven

Your light attracts me
It repels most people

But I see you for who you are,
*E*VANESCENCE
A MERE ILLUSION

ETHER

This vision became clear now
It's wrapped in my mind
And for all I know
The truth is what we bear to witness

Its inside of you
And inside of me
It's all we can ever be

God is everyone and everything

So tell me now
Do you see what I see?

CAMILA CARRILLO

LIGHT BEING

Humanity is of divinity not division
A creation made from source
Not apathy

Love is the truth
It's the answer
And the only thing that keeps us living

Embracing the touch of human connection
For a gentle moment of embrace

We crave this desire that inherits our momentary bodies
For an everlasting light that guides us every moment

Intertwined cosmically
A soul tribe
It's who were meant to be

ESSENCE

The beauty of life comes with its pain and truth of our shadow
The one we hide away for no one else to see
When there's so much more we have left to say

We meet others to recognize ourselves in different parts of them
In order to retain that part in us
Until we obtain those pieces so we can finally let them go

Fragility is often considered weakness,
still I believe it's never weak to remain soft and tender
In such a hard world we live in

CAMILA CARRILLO

INCARNATION

Shed your tears and promise me you'll never dwell
The power is hidden beneath the dark knight of our souls
Waiting for the sun to rise

Hidden identities are left to be found the moment we
    finally let our guards down.
Remaining broken in a broken world
While repairing ourselves in a junkyard full of memories

Open graves become closed doors
And open doors turn into graveyards of our past selves
Waiting to start again
Incarnating once more

APHORDITE

She's a dream and a nightmare
A woman and a child intertwined
Lady bird
With a withering mind

Entangled in muddy waters
Feminine so divine
Divinity and impurity
She's a goddess
She's a temptress
Everything you want to be

Graceless lady
High priestess so divine
Holy as can be

Unscathed, pure, and clean
Honey jar
Lips so sweet
Siren calls
Siren she
By the water
near the sea

Everything I want to be

CAMILA CARRILLO

PARIS, TEXAS

Summer revisits the past
It stays a while
and this time
I'm hoping it might last

Your return was the sweetest of them all

When we first met
A cool winter breeze swept in
Another year later
The sun is fading in and setting once more

Experiencing you
Is experiencing the seasons,
They come and go
Just like you do

WINGS YOU DESIRED

You gather my hear strings and tie them up
So you can keep them in your pocket
Somewhere safe for me

It reminds me of the feeling I felt in your arms,
Complete serenity

Summer days drift away and I can't make you stay

Free bird
Your just like me
I belong to no one
I've been searching for someone just like you

While you belonged to everyone

CAMILA CARRILLO

ILLUMINATION

When I see you
I see parts of myself too
I promise to die, so I can live again
This re-birth happens naturally

Crucify this pain inside me
Until I'm unable to feel
Swallow me whole
Then spit me out

Reel me in and devour me
I want to be yours

This body you hold so gently
A grace you carry so easily
May I protect you?
In between these blurred lines and solemn words I speak

You give me life
And I give you me

CHEMISTRY

You have a home in my heart,
A fire in my soul,
And a spark that burns those who try to touch it

"Tienes un hogar en mi corazon
Un fuego en mi alma
Y una chispa que quema a quien intenta tocarla."

TRANSUMITING

A release of stagnation
Fluidity and tears
Creating life for new energy that comes to shore
Washing away our impurities

So we can become pure again

CAMILA CARRILLO

FRAGMENTS

I am touched by the memory of every hand that's brushed
  its palms against mine
My skin and the warmth of my body

Every human willing to open the cage that holds their
  heavy heart
Knowing It may stay closed for long or open and willing
  to try once more

A smile that speaks unspoken words
Unable to erase
Becoming a core fragment in my bones

While ashes are all that remain

Why is it hard to understand?
This feeling we keep searching for
Already embedded within us

A love
A great escape
Something and someone, somewhere out there
That can never be replaced

RESURRECTION

Scars they heal
Wounds shall close
Every pain inside
Fuels a fire, everlasting
It never dies

Remnants that are existent
Some traces left behind

How could we long for suffering?
Dark is only darkness
Without its source of light

When the moon sets in
The sun will rise

Breathe again and breathe softly

    One last time

CAMILA CARRILLO

EPIPHANY

I'll forgive and forgive
Over and over again
Until my heart stops beating
And my blood turns from red to blue.
In a world that tries to turn me cold

I promise,
To keep you warm

FINALE

Each day I return to those who loved me
And those who left
Embracing our given duality
The good and bad
For all the ebb and flows

Nature has a way of speaking
And so, do we
I think there's a beauty in vulnerability
where words are never seen as weak

...

This is written for those who feel,
who love, who cry,
who laugh, who seek and live for others as much as they do for themselves
We live in an ever-changing world where it's never too late to start over and try again, because I promise you amongst this chaos there is bliss.

From my heart & soul,

Camila.

ABOUT THE AUTHOR

Camila Carrillo is an emerging author, poet, and artist dedicated to exploring the depths of human emotion and creativity. Embodying her commitment to self-expression.

Her debut collection, *Through the Eyes of a Flame: Poems of Past Loves and Past Lives*, delves into the complexities of the human experience with symbolic and metaphorical depth. Combining raw vulnerability with spiritual and esoteric undertones, her poetry invites readers to reflect on the resilience and beauty of the human spirit.

NOTES

USE THIS SPACE TO WRITE WHAT LINGERS

www.ingramcontent.com/pod-product-compliance
Lightning Source LLC
Chambersburg PA
CBHW020308010526
44107CB00001B/33